Freedom from Want

by Bryon Cahill

RED CHAIR
·PRESS·

Please visit our website at **www.redchairpress.com**.
Find a free catalog of all our high-quality products for young readers.

For a free activity page for this book, go to
www.redchairpress.com and look for Free Activities.

Freedom from Want

Publisher's Cataloging-In-Publication Data
(Prepared by The Donohue Group, Inc.)

Cahill, Bryon.
Freedom from want / by Bryon Cahill.
p. : ill. (some col.) ; cm. -- (The four freedoms)
Summary: The freedom from want is a right protected by the U.S. Constitution. Learn
why this right is important to young people today and explore how societies around the
world fare in supporting the critical basic needs of all of their citizens.
Interest age level: 009-012.
ISBN: 978-1-937529-93-2 (lib. binding/hardcover)
ISBN: 978-1-937529-85-7 (pbk.)
ISBN: 978-1-937529-98-7 (eBook)
1. Public welfare--Juvenile literature. 2. Right to food--Juvenile literature. 3. Right to
health--Juvenile literature. 4. Right to housing--Juvenile literature. 5. Public welfare.
6. Human rights. I. Title.
KF3720 .C34 2013

344.73/03   2012951569

Copyright © 2014 Red Chair Press LLC

All rights reserved. No part of this book may be reproduced, stored in an information
or retrieval system, or transmitted in any form by any means, electronic, mechanical
including photocopying, recording, or otherwise without the prior written permission
from the Publisher. For permissions, contact info@redchairpress.com

Edited by: Jessica Cohn
Designed by: Dinardo Design
Photo credits: Cover, title page, table of contents, p. 7, 10, 13, 15, 18, 26, 24, 28, 29: Dreamstime; p. 4: John
McConnico/AP Photo; p. 5: Moneta Sleet Jr./AP Photo; p. 6: FDR Library; p. 11: Craig Fry/AP Photo; p. 14:
Norman Rockwell; p. 15: AP Photo; p. 17: UN Photo/Marco Dormino; p. 19: Schalk van Zuydam/AP Photo;
p. 20: Sajjad Hussain/Getty Images; p. 21: Mohamed Sheiich Nor/AP Photo; p. 23: Morton Rostrup/AP
Photo; p. 24: Carl Brewer/AP Photo; p. 25: WHO; p. 27: Ron Jenkins/AP Photo

This series first published by:

Red Chair Press LLC   PO Box 333   South Egremont, MA 01258-0333

Printed in the United States of America

1   2   3   4   5   18   17   16   15   14

Table of Contents

The Meaning of Want

"I have the audacity to believe that people everywhere can have three meals a day for their bodies, education and culture for the minds and dignity, equality and freedom for their spirits.

—*Martin Luther King, Jr*

The year was 1964. Dr. Martin Luther King, Jr. won the Nobel Peace Prize. This award is given once a year to people who do great work in the name of peace. Dr. King won because of his efforts to bring freedoms to African American people.

Dr. King accepted the award in Oslo, Norway. There, he gave a speech. He said that he believed in a brighter tomorrow. There would be a day, he said, when no one would have to go hungry. People everywhere would be allowed to learn and enjoy life.

Dr. King was talking about the freedom from want.

Dr. Martin Luther King, Jr. was a civil rights leader. He gave a voice to African Americans who were fighting for their freedoms.

A Difficult Time

A world free of want is an ideal place. It is a goal that Dr. King talked about in the 1960s.

Years earlier, Franklin Delano Roosevelt talked about the same ideal or goal. Roosevelt, also called FDR, was the U.S. president from 1933 to 1945. During FDR's early years in office, many people in America did not have jobs. Some people were going hungry. They worried about how they would feed their families.

Nations in Europe were at war with each other. It was a difficult time for people around the world.

FDR spoke of Four Freedoms for all people in his January 6, 1941, speech to Congress.

Giving Hope

In January, each president makes a speech to **Congress**. Today it is called the State of the Union. The president goes over last year's events and sets goals for the year to come.

On January 6, 1941, FDR gave his speech. It was broadcast on the radio, so his words were heard across the U.S. and around the world. FDR knew that Americans feared going to war. But he wanted everyone to know that he thought some things were worth a battle. In his speech, he spoke of four important freedoms:

- Freedom of speech and expression
- Freedom of worship
- Freedom from want
- Freedom from fear

This famous speech became known as the Four Freedoms speech. It gave hope to millions of people.

Did You Know?

In 1941, FDR had been in office for eight years. At the time, many free nations in Europe were being taken over by Germany and Italy. The German and Italian governments of that time did not allow freedoms for all.

Freedom in America

""The third is freedom from want—which, translated into world terms, means economic understandings which will secure to every nation a healthy peacetime life for its inhabitants— everywhere in the world."

—Franklin Delano Roosevel

The U.S. **Constitution** was written when the nation was founded. It is the agreement that explains U.S. laws. It also talks about the role of government. The laws do not name the freedom from want. But the Constitution says that one of its purposes is to "promote general welfare."

All people need food, clothing, and a place to live. Freedom from want means no one should be without these basic needs. People work to pay for food and shelter. But some people cannot provide enough for themselves or their children. The laws of the U.S. say government must work in ways that help all people.

We the People of the United States, in Ord... domestic Tranquility, provide for the common defence, promote the general Welfare, ...Posterity, do ordain and establish this Constitution for the United States of Ame...

Article. I.

...n. 1. All legislative Powers herein granted shall be vested in a Congress of the Unite...
...resentatives.

...n. 2. The House of Representatives shall be composed of Members chosen every second...
...State shall have the Qualifications requisite for Electors of the most numerous Branch of the State...
...o Person shall be a Representative who shall not have attained to the Age of twenty five...
...shall not, when elected, be an Inhabitant of that State in which he shall be chosen.
...Representatives and direct Taxes shall be apportioned among the several States which may be i...
...s, which shall be determined by adding to the whole Number of free Persons, including those bo...
...d, three fifths of all other Persons. The actual Enumeration shall be made within three Year...
...thin every subsequent Term of ten Years, in such Manner as they shall by Law direct. The...
...ousand, but each State shall have at Least one Representative; and until such enumeratio...
...to chuse three, Massachusetts eight, Rhode-Island and Providence Plantations one, Conne...
...Delaware one, Maryland six, Virginia ten, North Carolina five, South Carolina five, and...
...When vacancies happen in the Representation from any State, the Executive Authority there...
...The House of Representatives shall chuse their Speaker and other Officers; and shall have the...
...n. 3. The Senate of the United States shall be composed of two Senators from each State, ch...
...shall have one Vote.
...Immediately after they shall be assembled in Consequence of the first Election, they shall be...
...nators of the first Class shall be vacated at the Expiration of the second Year, of the second C...
...the Expiration of the sixth Year, so that one third may be chosen every second Year; and if Va...
...the Legislature of any State, the Executive thereof may make temporary Appointments until...
...cancies.
...No Person shall be a Senator who shall not have attained to the Age of thirty Years, and been...
...n elected, be an Inhabitant of that State for which he shall be chosen.
...he Vice President of the United States shall be President of the Senate, but shall have no Vote,...
...e Senate shall chuse their other Officers, and also a President pro tempore, in the Absence of t...
...t of the United States.
...he Senate shall have the sole Power to try all Impeachments. When sitting for that Purp...
...no Person shall be convicted without the Con...
...tend further than to removal from Office, an...
...victed shall nevertheless be liable and subje...
...Manner of holding Elections for Senators and Representativ...
...or alter such Regulations, except as to the Pl...
...the Congress may at any time by Law make...
...The Congress shall assemble at least once in every Year, and such Meeting shall be...

The United States Constitution is the basis for the rules and laws for the country. Over the years, it has been updated, but not often.

People Needing Shelter

Over half a million people in America are homeless. Some people live on the street or in cars because they cannot find a job. Others work but still cannot afford a place to stay. Many of the homeless are children.

Homeless people may ask for money to buy food.

There are many reasons why people end up living without shelter. Housing can be expensive. Some people do not have family to live with. Others may be without a home for short periods. Natural disasters may destroy a family's home.

The U.S. government and other groups try to help the homeless. Free shelters provide a place to stay at night. And some cities have programs to give **temporary** jobs to homeless people.

WiLL WORK FOR FOOD

Helping the Homeless

The job of helping does not fall just on the government. Many people work to help those who live in want. For example, shelters give the homeless a place to sleep. The shelters get money from the government. But they also have support from people who pitch in to help. Soup kitchens and food pantries give food to the hungry. Many non-governmental organizations (NGOs) provide meals.

The Salvation Army is a well-known NGO that helps people in want. They have stores in towns across the U.S. People donate goods to be resold in the stores. Some of the money raised in the stores helps people who need food and shelter.

Did You Know?

The Salvation Army operates in 125 different countries.

Government Help

When people work, they pay taxes for unemployment services. These are services that the government provides. People who lose their jobs can sign up to be paid by the service. While a person looks for work, he or she can collect checks for a certain amount of time. This helps people pay for their housing, food, and clothing.

At some point, the unemployment service ends. When this happens, a person can ask for more help. For example, there is a service called the Supplemental Nutrition Assistance Program (SNAP). It is a **federal** program. SNAP gives people money to buy food. But it is not "real" money. SNAP offers something called food stamps. People can then use the stamps at grocery stores.

Did You Know?

In 2012, over 40 million Americans used food stamps to help feed their families.

Source: SNAP

Emergency Cases

When people do not
have proper food, shelter,
or medicine, their health
can suffer. Without the
right care, their health
problems can become
worse. People in want can
become very ill.

Many Americans pay
for health insurance.
Insurance is a pool of
money people share.
Having insurance helps
people pay bills when

In hospitals, doctors treat
some patients who have
no money to pay.

they get sick. It allows them to see doctors to keep
from getting ill in the first place. But there are some
people who do not pay for insurance. Many simply
cannot afford it.

A hospital must treat very sick people even if they
cannot pay. This is due to a law created in 1986. It is
called the Emergency Medical Treatment and Active
Labor Act. But this law covers emergency cases only.

The Art of Freedom

Norman Rockwell was a well-known artist. The work he did was popular during World War II. His art often shows the happy side of life in America.

In 1943, Rockwell made four famous paintings. They were first featured in a magazine called *The Saturday Evening Post*. Each painting shows one of the Four Freedoms in action.

One of these paintings is called *Freedom from Want*. It shows a family sitting at a table. It is Thanksgiving. Rockwell wanted to show the pleasure of family and having plenty to eat.

Rockwell's art was inspired by everyday American life.

About the Painting

Rockwell made more than three hundred paintings for *The Saturday Evening Post*. Some people think the Thanksgiving picture is the most famous.

In that same issue, a writer named Carlos Bulosan wrote about the painting. Here are a few lines from what he said:

"What do we want? We want complete **security** and peace. We want to share the promise and fruits of American life. We want to be free from fear and hunger."

All of these ideas can be found in the faces at the table in Rockwell's painting.

Did You Know?

At the end of 1941, the U.S. Congress set the 4th Thursday of November as the official day for Thanksgiving. It is on this day that Americans celebrate their freedom from want.

CHAPTER 2

Freedom Around The World

"Everyone has the right to a standard of living adequate for the health and well-being of himself and of his family, including food, clothing, housing and medical care…"

— *The Universal Declaration of Human Rights*

The United Nations (U.N.) is a group of 193 countries. Their goal is to work together for peace. They try to make life better for people around the world.

In 1948, the U.N. came to an agreement about the rights that all people should have. It is called the Universal Declaration of Human Rights. Like FDR's speech, it talks about the need for people to be free from want.

In many parts of the world, people are in want of food. For many years Somalia, an African nation, suffered a **famine**. But the U.N. worked to bring food to them.

The U.N. works every day to bring food to those who need it around the globe.

Finding Water

Many people in North America don't think about where water comes from. In most U.S. homes, water comes out of faucets. There does not seem to be a short supply of water.

People who get water so easily may find it hard to understand that water can be **scarce**. In some areas of the world, finding fresh water to drink and to bathe with is a big problem. In some places, water is harder to come by than food. The U.N. says that more than a billion people live in places where drinkable water is hard to find. That is one-fifth of the people in the world.

Did You Know?

Of all fresh water taken from underground wells or rivers and lakes in the U.S., only 1 percent is used by people at home to drink, cook, clean, or bathe with. *Source: US Geological Survey*

Unhealthy Water

Rwanda is a country in central Africa. Much of the water there is dirty. People can catch horrible diseases if they drink it. They can get sick just by taking a bath in it.

In some villages, people have to walk many miles to find a good water supply. They may spend all day going to a well or a fresh brook. Sometimes, children have to drop out of school just so they can help their families search for fresh water.

Getting water from the only well within miles is a daily activity in some places of the world.

Polluted Water

People who want for proper drinking water are more likely to suffer from diseases. Water that has germs in it can make people very sick. It can cause high fevers. It can even cause death.

Why would anybody drink unsafe water? In some parts of the world, that is the only choice. Years of poor living conditions, lack of rain, or unsafe industry can lead to polluted or dirty water. Nobody wants to drink unclean water. But many people have no other choice. They have to drink what is available.

India is a fast-growing country in Asia. Millions of people in India live without clean water.

Basic Needs

There are places in the world where sickness is a part of everyday life. Many areas do not have enough food and water. Or what they have is not good for them.

Underdeveloped countries suffer from a lack of services. They do not have clean water that comes through pipes. They may lack good roads or modern hospitals. Sadly, some people who live in underdeveloped countries want for many things. But first, and most importantly, they want to be healthy.

Holding their utensils, Somalis from southern Mogadishu wait to receive food.

Did You Know?

The U.N. declared the years from 2005 to 2015 as the "Water for Life Decade." U.N. Water is a group that is making people aware of the worldwide water crisis. They create better living conditions by bringing fresh water to areas that need it.

Helping Hands

"Do something. If it works, do more of it. If it doesn't, do something else."

—*Franklin Delano Roosevelt*

FDR was a president who believed strongly in helping those who are less fortunate. He knew that many people around the world want for basic human needs. He also thought that something should be done about it.

But the world's problems are not easy to fix. People who have the right resources and talents need to take action. Thankfully, many of them do.

There are many groups that work to help those with wants and needs. One such organization is called Doctors Without Borders. They set out to help those in need. Doctors from all over the world give their time. They travel to underdeveloped countries and give sick people the help and medicine that they need.

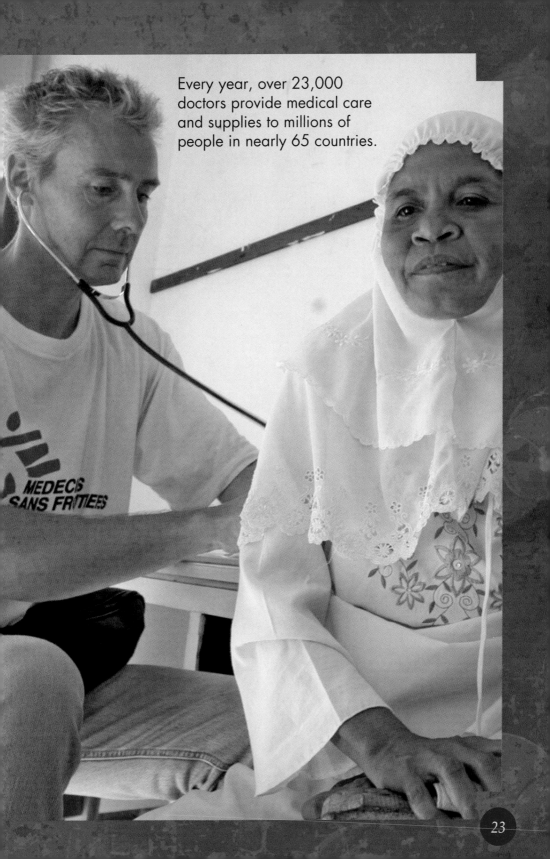

Every year, over 23,000 doctors provide medical care and supplies to millions of people in nearly 65 countries.

The mayor of Wichita, Kansas, (right) helps at a local food bank.

American Aid

In America, many groups give food to the hungry. Some of the groups are based in the towns where they work. Others are national. Feed America is just one example. This group works in all 50 states. The workers make sure that other people do not starve. Feed America brings food to many millions of people each year.

There are thousands of U.S. groups that help deliver food to people in want. There are also world organizations like the United Nations Children's Fund, or UNICEF. They work to give children around the world their basic needs.

Did You Know?

UNICEF gives aid to 190 different countries. They provide health care, clean water, good food, and education to underdeveloped nations.

Worldwide Action

Many other organizations work on a worldwide level. They give aid in the form of food, clean water, clothing, and medicine.

The World Health Organization (WHO) is a group that is run by the U.N. The headquarters for WHO are in the country of Switzerland. But there are 60 other countries that support the group. They do most of their work to improve public health in underdeveloped nations. But they do research to fight illnesses for all people.

Some children in India get help from the World Health Organization to stay healthy.

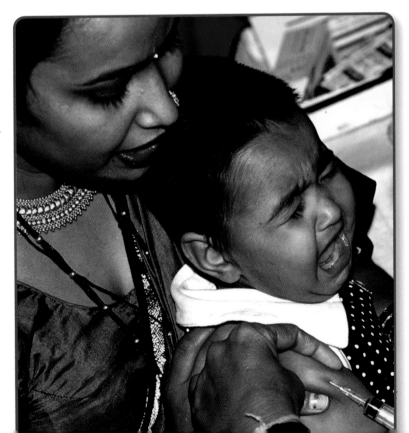

Freedom and Want

Freedom is a word that means many things to many people. If people are free, it means that they have control over how they live. A free man or woman can choose what to eat, what products to buy, where to go to school, and where to work.

Men and women who are free can take up hobbies, play sports, vote in elections, learn new ideas, and agree or disagree with other people. Being free means having the right to be the person you want to be.

There are different levels of freedom, though. A man who lives on the street and is often hungry may still have certain freedoms. But he may not have freedom from want. In fact, he may want many things. He may want a house, three solid meals a day, and health insurance. He may just want to feel comfortable, even if for one day. He is not free from the want of basic needs.

A woman who is free and has a house, nice clothes, plenty of food, and a car may still want other things. She may want better furniture or new clothes. This is not the type of want that FDR was describing in his Four Freedoms speech. A person who lives comfortably and safely does not want for basic needs.

If you have food to eat, clothes to wear, and a safe place to stay, you can be thankful for your freedom. Maybe someday you, too, can help those who are not yet free from want.

Exercise your freedom from want by being thankful that you have it and sharing your goods with others.

Did You Know?

Across the U.S., one of every four teens participates in community service or works with local charity each year. *Source: Volunteering in America*

Glossary

Congress law-making body of the U.S. government made up of the Senate and the House of Representatives

Constitution document that describes the supreme laws of the United States

famine extreme shortage of food

federal having to do with the national or central government

scarce hard to come by

security freedom from danger and risk

temporary lasting for only a limited period of time; not permanent

underdeveloped not advanced; having a low level of business and technology

In FDR's Words

In the future days, which we seek to make secure, we look forward to a world founded upon four essential human freedoms. The first is freedom of speech and expression—everywhere in the world. The second is freedom of every person to worship God in his own way—everywhere in the world. The third is freedom from want—which, translated into world terms, means economic understandings which will secure to every nation a healthy peacetime life for its inhabitants—everywhere in the world. The fourth is freedom from fear—which, translated into world terms, means a world-wide reduction of armaments to such a point and in such a thorough fashion that no nation will be in a position to commit an act of physical aggression against any neighbor—anywhere in the world. That is no vision of a distant millennium. It is a definite basis for a kind of world attainable in our own time and generation. That kind of world is the very antithesis of the so-called new order of tyranny which the dictators seek to create with the crash of a bomb.

—from FDR's address to Congress, January 6, 1941

Additional Resources

BOOKS

Caplan, Jeremy, and the Editors of TIME For Kids. *Franklin Delano Roosevelt: A Leader in Troubled Times.* New York, NY: HarperCollins, 2005.

Gunning, Monica. *A Shelter in Our Car.* San Francisco, CA: Children's Book Press, 2004.

Hubbard, Jim. *Lives Turned Upside Down: Homeless Children in Their Own Words and Photographs.* New York, NY: Aladdin, 2007.

Kaye, Cathryn Berger. *A Kids' Guide to Hunger and Homelessness: How to Take Action.* Minneapolis, MN: Free Spirit Publishing, 2007.

WEB SITES

Feeding America: *resources on the fight to end hunger*
http://www.feedingamerica.org

National Coalition for the Homeless: *projects, resources, and fact sheets*
http://www.nationalhomeless.org

U.N. Water: *Information on world water resources and use*
http://www.unwater.org

INTERACTIVE RESOURCES

Do One Thing: *End Homelessness Day, December 21*
http://www.doonething.org/calendar/endhomelessnessday.htm

Nobel Prize Video: *Martin Luther King, Jr. accepts award in 1964*
http://www.nobelprize.org/mediaplayer/index.php?id=1562

Unicef: *Games and activities promote global awareness*
http://youth.unicefusa.org/games

fdr4freedoms Digital Resource: *Videos, biographies, and interactive timeline*
http://fdr4freedoms.org

Note to educators and parents: Our editors have carefully reviewed these web sites to ensure they are suitable for children. Web sites change frequently, however, and we cannot guarantee that a site's future contents will continue to meet our high standards of quality and educational value. You may wish to preview these sites and closely supervise children whenever they access the Internet.

Index

Bryon Cahill has been writing for young people for over a decade. As editor of Weekly Reader's *READ* magazine, Bryon wrote short fiction, nonfiction, and reader's theater plays; created award-winning literary websites; and spearheaded an experimental theater adaptation of William Shakespeare's *Much Ado About Nothing* live on Facebook. An avid reader, Bryon also enjoys running and playing tennis at home in Morristown, New Jersey.